THE BIG-PICTURE REVISION CHECKLIST

How to Revise Your Novel the Easy Way

ALEX KOURVO

LOVELY DAY BOOKS

The Big-Picture Revision Checklist

Contents

1. The Good News About Revision — 1
2. Coming to Terms with Revision — 8
3. The Big-Picture Revision Checklist — 17
4. The Protagonist — 23
5. The Antagonist — 42
6. The Stakes — 57
7. The Five Big Scenes — 74
8. Beta Readers — 94
9. Getting to the Finish Line — 104
10. You Got This! — 111

Acknowledgments — 113
About the Author — 115
What's Next? — 117

The Big-Picture Revision Checklist: How to Revise Your Novel the Easy Way

Lovely Day Books

Copyright 2021 by Alex Kourvo

AlexKourvo.com

All rights reserved, including the right to reproduce this book or portions thereof except for brief quotes in reviews.

ISBN: 978-1-956107-03-6 (Hardcover)

ONE

The Good News About Revision

The adrenaline rush that comes with finishing a novel is like nothing else on Earth. It's an awesome high. You should be proud of what you've accomplished! Many writers start novels. Few finish them. With a finished draft in your hands, you're in an elite club. But those good feelings can also trip you up. You've worked so hard, for so long, it can make you think your novel is ready for publication, when it's really just the beginning.

Now is the time for revision. Which is *great* news. This is your chance to make your book as good as it can be. But it can also be intimidating. Where do you start? And how do you know when you're done?

When you're revising, you need to look at your novel differently than you do when you're drafting. When you write your first draft, you're looking at the novel from the inside out. You're with the characters in their world, seeing the story through their eyes. When you're revising, you're looking from the outside in. You're a neutral observer focused on the big picture. You'll need to step back and look at your novel as a whole, fixing the big issues first, before working your way down to smaller and smaller issues.

Many writers become paralyzed with indecision at this point. They don't know where to start, so they try to go in chronological order, making chapter one perfect before moving to chapter two, and then trying to make both chapters one and two perfect before moving on to three. This cycle repeats and repeats. Most of these writers never finish.

The worst thing you can do is open your manuscript at page one and start fixing awkward sentences and grammar mistakes. Or changing the word "sofa" into the word "couch" and the word "bucket" into the word "pail." Writers who jump directly into copyedits before doing the big-picture edits are looking for an easy way out. By staying busy at the sentence level, they never have to address the bigger issues that their novels have.

Copyedits are easy. English grammar has definitive rules, and everyone agrees on the right and wrong way to write a sentence. When we *do* break grammar rules in our writing, we break them deliberately, for effect, because we know how to use these tools.

Structural edits are hard. There are no absolute rules for things like character development, expression of theme, or direction of plot. No experts will agree on what makes the perfect novel, as there are too many variables. Writers strive to make the novel on paper match the vision of the novel in their heads, and the only definition of success is getting as close to that vision as possible.

The Second Draft is Magic

A novel is a big thing. It's too big to hold in your head all at once. Therefore, it's impossible for a novelist to write a completely clean first draft. Novelists who have written multiple books over many decades write rough drafts that are closer to finished than beginners do, but even they go back and change things before sending their books to editors.

The first draft is simply you telling yourself the story. The final draft focuses on language, making every sentence and paragraph as good as it can be. But it's the draft *between those two* that is the focus of this book. The middle draft is the heavy lifting draft. This is where you'll be moving stuff around and rethinking things.

The second draft is where the magic happens.

The Big-Picture Revision Checklist comes after you've completed your first draft. Fixing smaller issues like stilted dialogue or bland setting or overwrought description happens later, after you've finished your second draft. We're here to fix those big things that come between the first draft and the final one.

The only concerns in this middle draft are the big-picture issues. Using my twenty-point checklist, you'll improve things in a logical way, without endless loops through each chapter. You'll never be lost or overwhelmed, because your checklist will be there to guide you. This system will help you revise in an efficient way that will actually make the revision process easy and fun.

The *Big-Picture Revision Checklist* works for all

novels—literary and genre, middle grade through adult. These are general principles that will help all novels succeed. When you've gone through the whole checklist, you'll have a novel filled with characters that readers love, and you'll pit them against villains that readers hate. Your novel will have epic stakes with all the important scenes working to make the novel come to a smashing climax.

How I Can Help You

I have spent the last decade helping writers. I am an editor for small presses and private clients. I've taught over fifty workshops for aspiring writers, giving classes and workshops at libraries and writer's conferences. I have also read and reviewed over two hundred how-to books for writers. You can read all of the reviews on the Writing Slices blog.

I wanted to write *The Big-Picture Revision Checklist* because I haven't found another book that teaches this material. There are lots of books that will teach you how to write your first draft. There are lots of books on copyediting. But I haven't found any books that take a deep dive into that special middle draft, showing authors how to look at the big picture and revise their novels step-by-step.

The second draft is the draft that will make or break the novel. And yet, I couldn't find a book that gave the second draft the love it deserved. I wanted a book that would cut through the indecision and overwhelm, a book that would show authors how to revise their novels in a way that's easy and almost painless.

So I wrote one.

This is Your Job

If the middle draft is so important, why is it left up to writers? Isn't that the editor's job?

No, it's not. It's your job.

Professional editing is expensive. It's labor intensive and not something a computer can do, and therefore, it costs a lot. But too many authors hire an editor too soon in the process, wasting their money. An editor is not a ghostwriter. Her job is to help you improve what's already on the page. If what's on the page is half-baked, an editor can only do so much.

Think of an editor as rocket fuel. You bring an editor a complete rocket, with the engine in place and a solid body and all the working parts in order. Your editor puts it on the launch pad and lights it up. Next thing you know, your rocket is in space. (Publication! Reviews! Sales!) But if you bring your editor a half-finished thing, with pieces hanging off, and an unreliable engine, and some parts not sealed correctly, she can add all the rocket fuel in the world and that thing still won't fly. Adding more fuel won't help. It will just make a bigger fire on the launch pad as your rocket burns to a crisp.

Editors are worth your time and money, but only after you've done the heavy lifting yourself.

The Great Thing About Revision

I love the revision process and I hope you'll come to love it too. This is your second chance to make your book the best book it can be. With each draft you'll get closer and closer to that perfect vision in your head.

And it's not as hard as you might think. My twenty-point checklist is designed to eliminate frustration, needless repetition, and endless tinkering. Following the checklist step by step will keep you moving forward, always making progress toward a finished draft that will make you proud.

TWO

Coming to Terms with Revision

I f you thought that writing the rough draft of your novel was a rollercoaster of emotions, then buckle up. Revisions can be just as emotionally difficult as writing a rough draft. For one thing, you're finally getting to the heart of your story, the absolute core of it. In order to write a convincing book, you have to feel the emotions your hero feels, and there is no shying away from that. Readers know when you're faking it.

On top of that, writers sometimes feel like they're moving backwards. While writing your first draft, you could see your wordcount steadily rising, and every day, you made a little more progress. However, revision often means cutting words, not adding to them. Or at the very least, changing many of those beautiful words you've already put on the page. It's hard to tell yourself you're making progress when you're cutting and rearranging, crossing out whole passages, and making wild notes in the margins.

If your emotions are all over the place during the revision process, that's totally normal. Everyone feels this way.

Revision is Messy

Revision is hard for both plotters and pantsers. Plotters (people who worked with an outline) are used to writing chronologically, telling the story from start to finish, and they often find it difficult to revise scenes out of order. It can be hard to change or remove plot elements that disrupt their original vision. Pantsers (those who discover the story as they go) have a different problem. They have been up close and tight with the characters, looking at everything from within the story world. Taking a step back to look at the big picture often feels jarring.

Whether you are a plotter or a pantser, you need to make peace with the process. This shift in attitude will help you complete your revision. You need to accept that it's going to be messy for now, and that sometimes you have to make things temporarily worse in order to make them permanently better.

It can sometimes feel like you're playing the literary version of Jenga, where players take turns pulling a block out of the middle of the tower and stacking it on top. Small moves are okay, bigger moves are riskier, and one false move will make the entire thing collapse. Some writers are so afraid of ruining what they've already built that they don't want to make any changes at all.

Before you start revising, make a copy of your manuscript and tuck it away in an unused folder, so you have an untouched copy of the first draft while you make changes. If things go sideways, you can always go back to the original version. It's easier to start messing with things in version 2.0 if you know that the original still stands.

Revision is Overwhelming

The hardest part of revising a novel is right before you begin. For the first time, you're looking at the novel as a whole, which means you're looking at every single one of its flaws at the same time.

Let's say that you saw an insect in your house.

The Big-Picture Revision Checklist

Just one fly, or one little ant in your kitchen or perhaps a tiny spider. No big deal, right? You'd get the fly swatter and take care of it. Or, if you're nicer than me, you'd cup the bug in your hands and release it outside. You'd probably forget about it a few minutes later.

But let's say that you came home from work one day and your kitchen was overrun with ants crawling on the counters and the floor. Or what if there were suddenly five hundred spiders in your house? Or a thousand? You probably wouldn't even attempt to deal with them yourself. You would leave the house immediately and call an exterminator, because that problem is way too big for a homeowner to handle.

This is what revisions feel like when you're starting out. You're only going to handle one problem at a time, but it doesn't feel that way. Once you start, you're usually fine, but if you're having trouble starting, this is probably why. You're looking at too many problems at once.

As you go through this process, remind yourself that you didn't write every word of your book's first draft on the same day. You wrote one page at a time, and little by little, you got it done. You're going to do the same with your revisions.

And you'll have a checklist to help you.

Revision is Scary

This seems counterintuitive. After all, this is your chance to make your book better, so you'd think that writers would be eager to dive in. But many writers are actually afraid of this process.

One fear is that by changing things, you're going to make them worse instead of better. But you won't do that. Now that you can see the whole novel from start to finish, you know what will make it better. Besides, just by the act of finishing a draft, you've leveled up. You're a better writer now than when you started this book. You won't ruin it by revising it. (And you've saved a backup copy, just in case.)

But there are deeper fears than that. Revision is scary because the safety net is gone. When you were writing your rough draft and you made a mistake, you didn't care because you could always fix it in revisions. Now revisions are here. You had a second chance, and that second chance is now, and you have to do something about it. You either have to fix what's wrong or it will stay broken forever.

The other reason it's scary is because the more

you revise, the closer you get to putting your book out into the world for everyone to read—and to judge. Slowing down (or stopping) the revision process is one way to deal with that fear. I don't want to make too much of this, because of course, you can do as many drafts as you want. You can take all the time you need to revise. But I want to assure you that doubt and fear are normal at this stage.

Revision is Exhausting

Revision takes time. It's hard and it can be exhausting.

I recently did a revision of my own novel where I had to streamline things by making sure I didn't repeat myself. I spent the whole afternoon deleting some scenes and combining other scenes together. I sat in a comfortable coffee shop drinking a delicious latte, listening to great music on my headphones the whole time. And when I was done, I was so tired I could barely walk home.

Why was I so drained? I hadn't done any physical labor. I'd spent the day sitting on my butt deleting words. I should have been skipping home, not dragging the whole way.

But scientists who study the brain have learned that decision making is exhausting. The more decisions we make, the more tired we get. And what is revision other than a series of decisions?

Revisions always take longer than we want them to. If you've blocked out a certain amount of time to revise your first novel, double that. It's going to take longer than you think to get those words right, but I promise you, it will be worth it.

The First Step

Because of the mess, fear, overwhelm, and exhaustion, the first step in revising your novel should always be to walk away from it. Don't jump into revisions the split second you finish your rough draft. Come down from that emotional high of finishing a novel, make a plan, and then jump in.

Let it rest. Not for long—a week or so is all it takes to gain new perspective.

When you finish that first draft, celebrate! Go see a movie. Tackle that pile of books you've been meaning to read. Spend time with the friends you've been neglecting while you've been hiding in your writing cave. Clean your basement. Call your mom.

Or—my favorite—write something else. Write a short story, catch up on blog posts, or email a friend.

After this time away, you can start to evaluate your novel more objectively. You can start looking at it as a reader, not as the author.

You might think this isn't an efficient use of your time. Why waste a whole week or more letting the rough draft just sit there? But taking a small break between the rough draft and the revision will make revising so much easier. It will save you time in the long run.

The small window of time between drafts is also a good time to plan your revision. So many authors are disciplined when it comes to writing their first draft, but then think the revision will somehow magically take care of itself. You need to block out time for revision the same way you blocked out time to write your rough draft. Plan for healthy chunks of time when you can concentrate without interruption. Revision takes a tremendous amount of focus, and you're using a different skillset than you used to write the first draft. It's going to take every ounce of discipline and creativity you have to bring your novel to the finish line. Give yourself the time you need to do it right.

. . .

The Benefits of a Checklist

Having a checklist to follow will help deal with those churning emotions. It's a lot easier to deal with feeling scared or overwhelmed if you know you have a checklist to follow. You'll know you're taking care of everything, nothing will fall through the cracks, and you're improving your novel step by step. And if it gets a little messy along the way, so what? A checklist will help you tackle your revision methodically, starting with the most important issues. And a checklist will let you know when you're done! You won't get caught in the loop of endless tinkering. If you take care of every point on the twenty-point checklist, all of your big-picture revisions will be done and you'll have a solid second draft.

THREE

The Big-Picture Revision Checklist

You've come to terms with your revision process. You know it's going to take some time, and you know it's going to be hard, but you're prepared for this new journey. You've set realistic expectations, you've blocked out time on your calendar, and you've stocked up on coffee.

Now is the time to open your manuscript, and at the same time, open your mind. Parts of your rough draft need work. Other parts are excellent. But don't hold too tightly to the parts you like. Now is the time to consider making *big* changes. Writers often cling to storylines and character traits that aren't effective, simply because they worked so hard to think them up. But you need to trust that the same creative mind that came up with the original concept is equally capable of thinking of something better. Never be afraid to make changes—even big changes—if it means a better book.

The point of a checklist is to get an objective read on your manuscript. You want to start reading it like a reader, not as the author, with the distance you'll need to evaluate your manuscript. The twenty items on this checklist are the first twenty things an editor is going to look at when your book lands on her desk.

Don't Change All the Things!

I want to emphasize an important point. There are twenty items on this list, but it's very, very rare for a finished rough draft to need to fix all twenty of these things. I know I just told you to be brave and make big changes, but that does *not* mean you have to change every word you wrote. Chances are, you can look at your rough draft, and look at this list, and cross off most of these things, because you've already done them. You might need to work on ten things on this list. You might need to work on five. Or two.

So don't worry about the length of the list. And don't rip out the heart of your story based on a checklist. The list is an evaluation tool. You can think of it as a safety feature, like those pre-flight checklists pilots use. It's only meant to be used as a way to *make sure* that you've either done all these things or plan to do them in revisions.

The Big Picture

This draft is for stepping back and looking at the big picture, evaluating your novel as a whole. Now is not the time to get bogged down in making pretty sentences, or choosing the exact right word, or fixing spelling errors. That all comes later. Your brain will often try to get you to do the easier job of copyediting rather than the heavy lifting of structural edits. Don't let yourself get distracted or slowed down by those nitty-gritty details during this second draft.

A Note on the Examples

I learn best from examples, so I've used a lot of them throughout this book. I tried to use well-known novels such as bestsellers, award-winners, classics, and books that were made into movies. My hope is that most of these books are familiar to you.

When books are turned into movies, plots and characters often change from one medium to another. Some stories like *Ghetto Cowboy* and *Bird Box* were changed so much when they came to the screen that they're almost a different story. When I cite an example, always assume I'm referring to the novel.

Spoilers abound in these pages. It can't be helped. There isn't a good way to deeply analyze novels without revealing the plot twists. However, it's worth having a few books spoiled in the interests of learning.

The Twenty-Point Revision Checklist

Here are the twenty things to check when you're revising your novel. You must be able to answer *yes* to all of these questions. And bring receipts. What I mean is, it's not enough to think that you've done these things, or to have some vague sense that it's in your novel somewhere. You must be able to point to the exact page or pages where these things occur, and they must be explicit, not subtle. Until you can do that, don't send your book to beta readers, agents, or editors. And for goodness sake, don't publish your novel yourself

The Big-Picture Revision Checklist

until you're sure that every element of your story is working.

In later chapters, we'll look at each of these points in detail, but here is the complete list for your reference.

- Is your protagonist likable, or at least relatable?
- Is your protagonist flawed? Are those flaws the flipside of her strengths?
- Does your protagonist have a "save the cat" moment early in the book?
- Is your protagonist active?
- Does your protagonist change and grow?
- Does the antagonist have at least three scenes with the protagonist?
- Is the antagonist's motive clear?
- Is the antagonist stronger than the protagonist?
- Are your antagonist and your protagonist similar in some way?
- Is your antagonist ruthless?
- Does your protagonist have a clearly defined goal?
- Is this problem so big that it takes one

hundred percent of your protagonist's effort?
- Are there life-or-death consequences (of some kind) for failure?
- Is it impossible for the protagonist to quit?
- Are the stakes personal?
- Do you start your novel with a strong hook in the form of an active scene?
- Does your protagonist make a choice that leads him into act two?
- Is your midpoint scene full of action, emotion, and drama?
- Does your all-is-lost moment feel like a true defeat?
- Do you deliver your genre's version of an epic climax?

FOUR

The Protagonist

When you were writing the first draft of your novel, you were probably very focused on the plot. In order to make it to the finish line, you thought about things happening to your characters—or your characters making them happen. You felt like you knew your story people well enough and it was time to let them do all the things you imagined them doing. You thought about all the fun scenes you were eager to write, and the difficult scenes you dreaded. Or you thought about scenes that your genre demanded— the discovery of a dead body in a mystery, or the first kiss in a romance, or that first big chase scene in a thriller. That's fine for a first draft. In fact, it's crucial. But when we revise, the place to start is with the characters.

When we read a novel or watch a movie, we take the characters for granted, and we're here to see what happens to them. It's no wonder that we approach our own stories by first thinking about plot. But plot is extremely flexible. A plot can go in a hundred different directions, all of them equally good. However, for a character to be believable, she has to be consistent, with a rock-solid set of values and characteristics. She needs to know who she is, what she wants, and how far she's willing to go to get it. If you've nailed that, you'll have a much easier time with your plot.

Is your protagonist three-dimensional? Do his actions and motivations make sense? Readers want to be hooked by your story, they want to keep turning pages, but in order for them to do so, they need a reliable guide. They want to meet someone so interesting and engaging that they'll gladly go on a 300-page journey with him. Readers want to watch your hero or heroine change and grow through the story, ultimately ending up a better person than when the story began.

. . .

Is Your Protagonist Likable?

The first thing to consider about your hero or heroine is whether they are likable. It's not enough for the *author* to like the heroine. The *reader* has to like her. What are her good qualities? What can she do better than other people? What makes her relatable? What will make readers want to spend three hundred pages with her?

Many writers think they know the answers to these questions, but their answers are very vague. It's not enough to say that your hero is a nice person, or he's clever, or he has a good heart. You need to be able to point to the exact page in your manuscript that shows these qualities.

As authors, we love our protagonists. Often, they have a little piece of us in them. But you can't assume your reader will like your hero. *Show* the reader why they should fall in love with him. I can't emphasize this enough. From the first page, you need to show your hero being interesting and likable, or at least relatable. Figure out what makes your hero unique and then put that on the page. Don't just tell us that your hero is good with children, *show* him calmly breaking up a playground spat while making the children feel valued and heard. Don't just tell us that your hero is selfless, *show* him volunteering at the homeless shelter on Saturday mornings, even though he'd rather sleep in.

Some protagonists are so beloved that readers will happily read about their many adventures through multiple novels—even if the plots are essentially the same from book to book. Stephanie Plum is a heroine who millions of readers have followed through more than twenty novels by Janet Evanovich.

Stephanie Plum is sassy, she's independent, and she's got a whole lot of love for her wacky family. In *One for the Money*, the first book in the series, Stephanie loses her job as a lingerie buyer at a department store. Now, she's trying to be a bounty hunter, and she's hilariously bad at it. Still, she's determined to prove herself, even though she's so afraid of her own gun that she keeps it hidden in her cookie jar.

In *Ghetto Cowboy*, by G. Neri, Cole is a 12-year-old from Detroit whose single mother sends him to Philadelphia to live with his dad. Cole's dad runs an urban stable, and loves horses more than people. At first, Cole wants nothing to do with the four-legged beasts.

Cole is an outsider in the world of urban riders.

But he's smart and a good observer. He quickly sizes up situations and people. He asks a lot of questions, and that honest innocence endears him to readers. He eventually bonds with an abandoned horse that no one else can tame. Cole knows what it's like to be abandoned, since neither of his parents seem to want him, and he taps into that inner feeling to find the courage to approach a frightened horse. Once he has that horse, he's loyal to the end.

Authors often get rejection letters from agents or editors that say, "I didn't connect with this," or "this just didn't work for me," or "I didn't love this enough." Like all rejection letters, this might sound frustratingly vague, but take another look. When an agent says, "I didn't connect with this," what she's really saying is, "I didn't connect with the *protagonist*."

If readers believe in the heroine, and care about her success, they will eagerly turn pages through any number of plot twists. Readers will even forgive a less-than-stellar plot if they love the hero or heroine, but the reverse is not true. The way to make them care about your main character is to make that character as likable and relatable as you can.

. . .

Is Your Protagonist Flawed?

But be careful that you don't make your heroine too perfect. Nobody wants to read about a character who always looks beautiful, always does the right thing, is so sexy that they have the partner of their choice, and is beloved by everyone at work, at home, and in the community.

Readers want to watch your heroine change and grow. She can't do that if she's a perfect person who never makes mistakes. Many writers know this but they're unsure what kind of flaws to give their heroine, so they start giving their protagonist random flaws that sound quirky or fun. Maybe she should be bad at cooking? Dances like something from a zombie movie? Doesn't get along with her mother? Flaky? Clumsy? Gets lost all the time? Maybe she should talk non-stop? Or lose her temper easily?

Don't do this. Don't start giving your heroine random flaws. You want her to be a well-rounded person, but if the flaws come from nowhere, it will seem contrived. The ideal place to look for your heroine's flaws is in her *strengths*. You've already given your heroine positive qualities. Now turn those on their heads. The only flaws that matter are the ones that come directly from her best qualities.

The Big-Picture Revision Checklist

Everything you like about your hero has a downside. Use it.

In *One for the Money*, Stephanie is sassy and independent, which means she's also rude, and she doesn't ask for help when she really should. At one point she ends up naked, handcuffed to her own shower curtain rod—a situation that could have been prevented if she'd asked for help. She loves her wacky family, which means she lets them get away with some pretty bad behavior. And that gun in her cookie jar? Well, it's hard to be a badass bounty hunter if you leave your gun at home.

Janet Evanovich has done a wonderful job of making sure that all of Stephanie's strengths go hand-in-hand with her weaknesses.

In *Ghetto Cowboy*, Cole's best qualities are the ones that get him into trouble the most. His innocence tips into gullibility, as he lets other people take advantage of him. He's smart, but not as smart as he thinks he is, and he often does things without considering the consequences. He steals a horse that's been impounded by the city, even though he doesn't have any way to feed or care for it. He hangs around his cousin, even though he knows his cousin is dealing drugs, because he's too loyal. He can size up situations quickly, but he just as often gets them wrong, like when he assumes his dad doesn't want him, when the truth is, his dad loves him so much he's terrified of messing things up.

You can give your hero any strengths. You can give him any flaws. But it's crucial that you make one the flip side of the other. If you want to make a well-rounded character who readers will believe in, you need to make these positive and negative qualities mirror one another. When you're revising, look at your heroine's personality and make sure that every flaw has a bright side, and every strength has a cost.

Save the Cat

Every novel needs to include a moment in the first few chapters where the heroine does something small, kind, and a little bit self-sacrificing. Blake Snyder calls it a "save the cat" moment and that name has spread through the writer community. A save the cat moment is vital to your novel. More than anything else, this is the one thing that will bond your reader to your hero.

The save the cat moment doesn't have to be big, and it doesn't have to tie into the main plot. In fact, it's probably better when it doesn't. You want to give the reader a clear signal that your hero is a good person, and therefore it doesn't count if the plot forced him into it.

Let's look at something that is *not* a save the cat moment. In *The Hunger Games* by Suzanne Collins, Katniss Everdeen lives in a world where teenagers are randomly chosen to fight to the death on live TV in order to secure food and resources for their towns. When Katniss' little sister is chosen for the Hunger Games, Katniss volunteers to take her sister's place. Some people point to that as her save the cat moment, but it's not. It's too big. It alters the trajectory of the plot completely. Besides, what choice did Katniss have? Her sister is only twelve, while most of the fighters are sixteen and up. Katniss is a trained hunter, while her sister has never lifted a weapon. When Katniss yells that iconic line, "I volunteer as tribute!" that scene is doing other important jobs in the book, but it's not saving a cat. The save the cat moment should be selfless like this, but not in a life-altering way.

It also can't be too small. Holding a door open for someone doesn't count. Helping to pick up schoolbooks that the bully has knocked out of the nerd's hands is too easy. Anyone can do those things. Instead, find a small kindness that's unique to your hero. What kind thing does your protagonist do because only he can? Have him perform that action, and then don't mention it again. Even if the reader notices it, the hero does not. And certainly don't let your hero pat himself on the back, or think highly of himself for doing it. For a save the cat moment to be truly effective, the hero shouldn't think of it as anything out of the ordinary. This kind of everyday heroism comes naturally to him, simply because of who he is.

Katniss Everdeen's save the cat moment comes in the first chapter, when she and her friend Gale forage strawberries and then sell them to the mayor. The mayor's daughter has a new dress, because today is the day that a teenager will be chosen for the Hunger Games, and everyone wears their best clothes for the occasion. Gale takes a dig at the mayor's daughter, because he's resentful that as a rich kid, she's less likely to be chosen than he is. However, Katniss defends her. Katniss reminds Gale that it's the system that's at fault, not this one person. The mayor's daughter is just a kid, and is as powerless to change the system as they are. This is a small moment, but Katniss is willing to call out her best friend for bad behavior, and does it in defense of someone who isn't her friend. She didn't have to do it. The mayor would have bought the strawberries regardless, and she could have kept the peace with Gale. But it shows what kind of person Katniss is. She tells the truth even when it hurts, and she has a very clear understanding of how broken their society is and what needs to change.

A save the cat moment can be almost anything. It can be helping a neighbor who is too frail to shovel her own walk, doing extra work when a co-worker is having a hard time, helping a stranger find her way, find the bus stop, or find her lost dog. However, whatever you choose not only has to be small, kind, and self-sacrificing, it also has to fit the theme and tone of the book. A funny save the cat won't fit in a serious novel. A very mature save the cat won't fit in a middle grade book. A sticky-sweet romantic save the cat is not appropriate for a horror novel. Look at other novels in your genre, and follow the road map that other authors have laid out.

Finding the perfect save the cat moment isn't easy. You can't let it be too subtle or readers won't notice it. You can't let it be too obvious or readers will catch on to what you're doing. You want your save the cat moment to fit seamlessly into your novel so readers will start to love your hero without ever asking themselves why.

In *To All the Boys I've Loved Before* by Jenny Han, Lara Jean Covey is a high-school junior who writes love letters to all her crushes, but doesn't send them. Lara Jean's older sister is very responsible and her younger sister is a brat. However, her older sister has gone overseas for college, leaving Lara Jean in the role of eldest sister. When her younger sister is angry at her for no good reason, Lara Jean goes out of her way to bake her sister's favorite cookies and sneaks them into her room, hoping to make peace with her.

This is a great save the cat moment because it fits the story. It's not huge. It's just a batch of cookies, and Lara Jean herself doesn't think much of it. But at this moment, Lara Jean values her sister's hurt feelings over her own feelings of being right. She's willing to lose an argument for the sake of family harmony. It's a sign of maturity in a young woman who is struggling with growing up, so it fits very well into the YA genre. It's also ironic, since her little sister later sneaks into Lara Jean's room, finds the secret love letters, and mails them.

Did you ever give a novel a three-star review because it was just sort of...meh? I'm talking about a novel that was entertaining enough to hold your interest, but rather forgettable once you were done. It was fine, but you had no regrets when you put it in the charity bin rather than pass it on to a friend.

Pause. Take that book out of the donations pile. Go back to the first few chapters and try to find the save the cat moment. Bet you can't find it, because it's probably not there. And the reason the book was only so-so is because you never bonded to the heroine, so you didn't truly care about her adventures.

Your Protagonist Must be Active

Make sure that your heroine is acting, not just reacting. If your plot has the heroine doing nothing more than reacting to problems that are thrown at her, you've got some rewriting to do. She may be reacting to unfolding plot events, but she should still have a clear goal in mind. Make sure she *wants* things. She's making decisions. She's trying.

Usually, at the beginning of the novel, new problems are coming at your heroine faster than she can solve them. It's okay if she starts running as fast as she can just to stay in place. But sooner rather than later, we need to see her come up with a plan and then execute that plan.

In *The Martian* by Andy Weir, astronaut Mark Watney is doing whatever it takes to survive alone on Mars, making plan after plan, some of which work and some of which do not. He figures out his shelter, then soil to grow potato plants from the rations left behind, then how to synthesize water. But in making water out of oxygen and hydrogen, he accidentally leaves free-floating hydrogen in his habitat, which explodes on him. Once he gets his shelter, air, water and food under control, he starts planning ways to contact Earth and how to drive across the Martian terrain to the pick-up point.

It's a long, hard process, and there are many times that Watney makes mistakes that could get him killed. But he always has one more thing he can try, and he won't rest until he's back home. And because he's trying so hard, every single person on planet Earth is rooting for him.

In *The White Tiger* by Aravind Adiga, the hero, Balram Halwai, was born into an extremely poor family in rural India. Balram wants desperately to improve his lot in life, so he schemes and finesses his way into a job as a chauffeur for a wealthy, corrupt man. Balram does everything he can to rise in the servant hierarchy, but plain old hard work will simply keep him where he is. To truly get anywhere, he also has to inflate his resume, betray other servants, pay bribes, and spy on his employer.

Balram never lets himself be satisfied with the status quo. He's always thinking about the next rung on the ladder. He makes lots of blunders, including withholding money he promised to send back to his family in the village and angering his grandmother, who as the matriarch of the family, still holds power over him from afar. He turns his back on the other drivers in his social circle instead of making them allies, cutting himself off from valuable help.

Balram's single aim is to get himself out of servitude, one scheme at a time. And because he's always actively pursuing his goal, readers root for him to succeed.

When you're revising your novel, ask yourself how many mistakes your hero makes. The answer should be "a lot." In fact, the more mistakes he makes, the better. You've got a flawed hero trying to solve a problem he's never faced before. Of course he's going to make mistakes. But readers would much rather see a hero try and then fail than never try.

. . .

How Has Your Protagonist Changed?

All of this trying and failing and making mistakes means that your heroine is going to grow and change throughout the novel, which is exactly what your readers want to see.

She's got a big problem to solve, one that means a lot to her. She was thrust into a new adventure, and took steps toward solving the main conflict. By the end, she should be a different person than when the story started.

The novel *Jaws* by Peter Benchley is about a small resort island terrorized by a killer shark. The protagonist, Sheriff Brody, begins as an outsider. He's not a native of the island, he's uncomfortable with the town, and he's even afraid of the water. By the end of the novel, he's a badass shark hunter. He's literally swimming with the sharks. Moreover, he has become a true resident of Amity Island, accepted by the townspeople. It's an amazing transformation, and the reader can clearly see it on the page.

In *Bird Box* by Josh Malerman, creatures from another dimension have come into our world and if a human sees one, she will kill everyone around her and then kill herself. People adapt to this new reality by staying indoors behind blackened windows, always wearing blindfolds on the rare times they venture outside.

The heroine, Malorie, starts out the novel as a 24-year-old who hasn't quite got her life figured out yet. She's living in an apartment she can only afford because she shares it with her sister, she works a dead-end job, and she's pregnant because of a one-night stand. When the creatures come and her sister kills herself, Malorie finds her way to a home of survivors, but she never takes a leadership position, and simply goes along with whatever her housemates want. She's scared of everything.

By the end of the novel, she has become a completely different person. She's been in charge of two children, raising them completely on her own for four years, and it's made her tough, strong, and brave. She's trained herself and her children for a journey by boat to a safer place. She knows exactly what she must do in order to succeed, even if it means being a terrible mother by the standards of the world before. As she rows the boat, she remembers the young woman she once was, and all the things that got her to this place. The Malorie from four years ago could never take this journey. The Malorie of today can. She understands how much she has changed, and the reader does too.

As you're revising, look for places where you can contrast the old with the new. Pick out details that reveal this new side to your character. It's not enough to simply *tell* readers that the heroine has changed. Give the reader specific details that paint a before-and-after picture. It's not enough that the heroine thinks she's different now, or that she feels different. She has to do something to *show* that she's not the same person that she was when the story began.

The Special Case of Antiheroes

Antiheroes are becoming more popular. But don't forget the "hero" part of antihero. There must be something about him that readers enjoy if they're going to spend an entire novel with him. Is he funny? Protective? Loyal? Fearless? An antihero believes that idealism and morality are for other people, and he loves to call out hypocrisy, but he does have a personal code he lives by. Unlike a true villain, an antihero has lines he won't cross. He's not unscrupulous so much as pragmatic, believing that the ends justify the means.

An antihero is usually a realist who has almost, but not quite, given up on humanity. That *almost* is very important because there's always something or someone that the antihero believes in. The eleven-book *Burglar* series by Lawrence Block is about a burglar named Bernie Rhodenbarr who steals things on commission, or when the opportunity arises, or just because he can. He also has to prove himself innocent of murder time and again because dead bodies always show up at his burglary sites. Bernie is a cynical, judgmental criminal who uses people. You probably wouldn't want to hang out with him in real life. But he's a wonderful companion for a novel, because he's clever, funny, and loves his cat, his best friend Carolyn, and the cute bookstore that he runs as a front. He only steals things that are easily replaceable or heavily insured. Besides, the cops are so much worse than Bernie will ever be, leading the reader to wonder who the true criminals are.

Antiheroes are a tough sell, but it helps if you can find the one quality that readers can relate to. Emphasize that quality over and over. Make your antihero understandable, sympathetic, and fun, and readers will happily follow his adventures—and even root for him to win.

FIVE

The Antagonist

Now it's time to turn your attention to the antagonist of the story. It's important for the hero's actions and motivations to make sense, but it's *crucial* that the antagonist's do so.

If you think of your plot as a car, the heroine is the driver. She's the one that's steering, deciding at every turn where the story will go. The antagonist is the engine. It's the antagonist who provides the energy for the forward movement of the story. The antagonist is constantly challenging the heroine, disturbing her routine and bringing her out of her comfort zone. Without the antagonist's energy and effort, the plot would go nowhere, and the heroine would happily stay at home.

This is true of an antagonist who is the classic bad guy in thrillers, such as the terrorist, the murderer, or the banker who funds an arms dealer. It's also true of the antagonist in literary novels, such as parents, siblings, romantic rivals, or someone trying to ruin the heroine's career. No matter the genre, the reader needs to see the antagonist on the page, understand his motive, and see him get his comeuppance at the end.

Three Scenes

A villain you can't see is a villain you can't fight. Which is why in every novel, the antagonist needs to reveal himself early. Make sure your hero and your antagonist have at least three scenes together, one in each act. More is better, but three is the minimum. If your antagonist stays in the shadows, or shows up very late in the novel, it will drain that vital energy from your story. The protagonist will still be in the driver's seat, but he'll be spinning his wheels, going nowhere.

The Silence of the Lambs by Thomas Harris is about FBI trainee Clarise Starling, who is matching wits with death row prisoner Dr. Hannibal Lecter. Clarise needs Hannibal's help in solving a new case, so she visits him in prison, looking for information. He gives her a single clue and sends her on her way. Clarise is forced to return to the prison again and again, and each time, Hannibal only gives her a sliver of the information she needs. This was a deliberate choice on the author's part. Thomas Harris could have set up his plot so that Clarise visits Hannibal a single time, gets him to tell her everything she needs to know, and goes on to solve her current case. But instead, Hannibal holds back as much as he can, Clarise has to tease out every clue, and each visit to the prison is more tense than the last.

In *The Hundred Foot Journey* by Richard C. Morais, the Haji family has moved from India to France and have opened a casual Indian restaurant across the street from a fancy French restaurant. The Haji family are the big-hearted heroes, while the French restaurant is run by closed-minded bigots. But it's not enough for the two restaurants to compete for customers. The author makes sure the chefs and staff interact directly time and again. They attempt to steal one another's menus. They try to beat one another to the farmer's market for the freshest produce. Noise and smells drift across the street. The French chefs spray racist graffiti on the Indian restaurant and even try to burn it down. It's the constant clash between the insiders and the newcomers that makes for a full, rich novel.

It's harder in a classic murder mystery, where the big reveal of the killer comes at the climax. But even there, the detective is fighting the *forces* of the bad guy. The harder she tries to uncover clues, the harder the killer tries to cover his tracks. There are lies, misdirection, and red herrings. And there is almost always a second murder at midpoint, to eliminate a witness when the detective gets too close. Every time the detective gets closer to the answer, the villain throws up a new roadblock to the investigation.

The important thing to remember is that this is a deliberate choice that you, the author, are making. In real life, we avoid people who make us uncomfortable. In fiction, the bad guy is ever-present and always seems to be in the protagonist's face. Do whatever you can to get your protagonist and your antagonist on the page as often as possible.

Does Your Antagonist Have a Good Motive?

Does the antagonist have a reason for doing what she does? Nobody is simply evil. Humans do things for specific reasons, and those reasons are universal—money, success, safety, power, love. The same kinds of things that motivate a heroine will also motivate her rival. Ask yourself why your antagonist is doing what she does. These don't have to be particularly good reasons, or honorable ones, but they do have to be clear to the reader.

In *Misery* by Stephen King, antagonist Annie Wilkes is absolutely certain that the world needs a new novel from hero Paul Sheldon. She's certain that his novel will make the world a better place, and she's determined to hold Paul prisoner until he delivers the exact book she wants. This seems ridiculous to most of us, but it makes perfect sense to Annie Wilkes.

Some editors say that an antagonist should be so sympathetic that you could outline the entire novel from his point of view. I think that's taking things too far. An antagonist's motives don't have to be completely understandable to the reader. After all, the antagonist is usually a bad person and the reader (we hope) is not. However, even if the reader doesn't sympathize in any way with the antagonist, she has to believe, one hundred percent, that the villain will stop at nothing to get what he wants. Your job as a writer is to convince the reader that the antagonist has such deep-seated reasons for what he does that he will never waver in his pursuit.

In *The Underground Railroad* by Colson Whitehead, the antagonist, Arnold Ridgeway, is determined to recapture the heroine, Cora, and return her to the plantation from which she has escaped. Ridgeway is a murderous psychopath whose racism and hatred are part of his identity. Joining the slave patrol is a natural fit for him. The reader doesn't need to understand what's in Ridgeway's heart. We don't need to sympathize with him in any way, because how could we? But the reader needs to understand why Ridgeway is so dogged in his pursuit of Cora. What is one enslaved person amongst so many? Why does he single her out and why will he never, ever give up?

Years before, Cora's mother also ran away from that same plantation. The local patrol wasn't able to find her, so they called in a specialist—Ridgeway. He wasn't able to find Cora's mother either and it's a blot on his record. When Cora runs away as well, Ridgeway takes it personally, and he's determined to find her at any cost. He pursues her through Georgia and the Carolinas, even into Indiana, and the only thing that will stop him is his own death.

Not all motives are bad or selfish ones. Sometimes antagonists are motivated by love. Weird, huh? How can an antagonist be motivated by *love*? But in some literary novels, family epics, and women's fiction, the antagonist does all the wrong things, but he thinks he's doing it for the hero's own good.

The Joy Luck Club by Amy Tan is about four women who have emigrated from China and become friends now that they are living in San Francisco. They are all raising daughters, and trying to instill traditional Chinese values in them, even though their daughters are fully American and don't understand or appreciate their mothers' old-fashioned ways. The daughters rebel in ways big and small, from refusing to go to Chinese language lessons to refusing to marry Chinese men. The mothers are exasperated and clamp down harder, because they truly fear for their daughters. To them, the old ways are the best ways, and letting their daughters be like Americans is unthinkable.

But Tan also shows the mothers' side of the story. Through flashbacks of the mothers' lives in China, the reader comes to understand why these "unreasonable" women are the way they are, and that they have each made amazing sacrifices for the daughters they love so much.

As you're revising, take another look at your antagonist. Why is she the way she is? Why does she feel justified in what she's doing? Are those reasons clear to the reader? How can you show the antagonist's motives on the page?

Is Your Antagonist Stronger Than Your Protagonist?

An antagonist needs to be stronger than the hero, at least at first. Throughout the novel, the hero will be challenged time and again, leading to his growth and change. In video game terms, the hero will "level up." Therefore, at the outset, the scales should be wildly imbalanced in the villain's favor.

This is easy to see when it's a thriller, science fiction, or fantasy. Whoever has the bigger guns or the best magic is on top. In *The Lord of the Rings* by J.R.R. Tolkien, Sauron is the powerful, evil king of Mordor, who wants to rule all of Middle Earth. Sauron has armies of orcs at his bidding, and appears as an all-seeing eye that constantly watches his subjects. He's so powerful that some kings surrender to him right away, without a fight, because it's better than watching their kingdoms be completely destroyed. How can a small hobbit like Frodo, with only a handful of allies, hope to win against him? The two are so unevenly matched that the reader has no expectation that Frodo can achieve his goal of destroying the cursed ring of power. And in fact, it takes three thick books for Frodo to do so, with many defeats and setbacks along the way.

But what about other genres like literary fiction, YA, women's fiction, or historical fiction? You absolutely can (and must) weigh the scales in favor of the antagonist, no matter what genre you're writing in. Sometimes it's an imbalance in structural power, like a student and a teacher, or an employee and a boss. Sometimes it's parent and child.

Sometimes one party has higher social standing, as in the novel *Legally Blonde* by Amanda Brown, where California party girl Elle Woods is shunned by the old-money kids at Harvard. Or in *Dork Diaries* by Rachel Renée Russell, where the protagonist is a poor scholarship student in a middle school where the girl at the top of the social ladder tries to ruin her life. In *The Hundred Foot Journey* by Richard C. Morais, the antagonists have a much stronger standing in the community than the Haji family. The French restaurant has a Michelin star and a devoted fan base, while the entire town distrusts the newcomers. On the Indian restaurant's opening day, it's empty. The Haji family has a huge uphill climb for social acceptance.

Are Your Protagonist and Your Antagonist Similar?

Are your protagonist and your antagonist similar in some way? This might seem like a silly question. You've worked hard to make your heroes as good as possible and worked equally hard to make your bad guys bad. However, the strongest protagonist/antagonist duality is when the hero and the villain are two sides of the same coin.

In *The Lord of the Rings: The Two Towers* by J.R.R. Tolkien, Frodo's main antagonist is the gollum Smeagol. The nasty little creature is supposedly Frodo's guide to Mount Doom, but he's leading Frodo astray at every turn. Frodo's companion sees right through Smeagol and wants to ditch him, but Frodo pities him. He realizes that it's the power of the cursed ring—the ring that Frodo himself now carries—that's made Smeagol what he is. Smeagol was once a hobbit just like Frodo, and if Frodo isn't careful, he'll end up the same way.

In the Sherlock Holmes stories by Arthur Conan Doyle, the villain that readers remember most is Moriarty. He makes a fascinating foil for Holmes because the two characters are almost exactly alike. They are both sociopaths with a huge intellect, and a driving need to use that intellect to influence the world. But Sherlock uses his powers for the greater good, while Moriarty uses his for selfish gain.

Sometimes writers give the heroine and her nemesis a similar background or a similar love object. Sometimes they look the same. Sometimes it's similar names. Think of Valjean and Javert in *Les Misérables* or Andi and Miranda in *The Devil Wears Prada*. These names were not a coincidence. The authors were giving the readers a huge clue, telling the reader to pay attention to the similarities between these two characters.

You don't have to overdo this. Some stories lend themselves to these parallels more easily than others. However, make sure there is a piece of the protagonist in the antagonist and vice-versa. Think of a yin-yang symbol, where there is a dot of black on the white half and a dot of white on the black half. In some tiny way, the reader has to wonder why one of these characters went good while the other went bad.

Make Your Antagonist Ruthless

In fact, your hero and your villain can be almost one hundred percent alike, except for one crucial detail, and it's that detail that makes all the difference. How far are they willing to go to get what they want? Your heroine and your antagonist are both after an important goal. They are both determined to get it. They are both willing to make great sacrifices to achieve their goal. The difference is, the antagonist will sacrifice other people, while the hero will sacrifice himself.

The hero's actual life doesn't have to be on the line, although that's an option. The hero can also sacrifice his career, his romantic relationship, his fortune, his freedom, or his social standing. He'll give up whatever is necessary to achieve his goal. The antagonist isn't willing to do that. Selfishness is part of the villain's makeup, and often what leads to his downfall.

But other people are fair game for the antagonist. To the antagonist, other people are simply a means to an end. How many times in thrillers do we see the villain casually kill one of his own henchmen?

The hero, however, isn't willing to sacrifice even one other person, and will often go out of his way to protect others. Even worse, the antagonist *knows* this about the hero. The antagonist knows there are lines the hero will not cross, people he will not harm, and the antagonist uses this against the hero. This is part of what makes the antagonist stronger than the hero. The antagonist has tools the protagonist refuses to use.

In *The Lion, The Witch, and the Wardrobe* by C.S. Lewis, the land of Narnia is ruled by the White Witch, who has kept the land in perpetual winter, since she cares nothing for her subjects. She has a garden filled with servants and enemies she's turned into stone. When the four Pevensie children accidentally travel to Narnia, the White Witch charms one of the younger children named Edmund, promising him food, sweets, and power. He initially betrays his siblings in loyalty to the witch, and when he tries to rejoin their side, she tries to kill him.

However, the savior of Narnia, the lion Aslan, takes Edmund's place and sacrifices himself instead. The White Witch is perfectly willing to kill anyone to get what she wants, even those who are loyal to her, and she also knows that Aslan—her true target—will gladly give his life for the child's.

This dynamic is found in literary novels as well. John Willoughby is one of the villains in *Sense and Sensibility* by Jane Austen. Willoughby flirts with Marianne, making romantic promises to her he has no intention of fulfilling. One day, he abruptly leaves for London, breaking all contact, leaving Marianne with a broken heart. Only later does she find out what a scoundrel he truly is. He seduced a fifteen-year-old girl and abandoned her when she became pregnant. Upon hearing this news, Willoughby's aunt disinherits him, leaving him broke and in debt. Willoughby then decides to turn his fortunes around by marrying the richest woman he can find. He ends up married to a wealthy woman he doesn't even like.

To Willoughby, people (especially women) are merely a means to an end, and he'll use anyone in order to increase his fortune and maintain his social standing. Moreover, he knows that a "gentleman" can get away with this behavior, because his social circle runs on politeness, always sweeping scandal under the rug. As long as he's outwardly polite, and observes all the social niceties, he will never be publicly called out for the things he does.

As you're revising your novel, find places to give your heroine the moral high ground by showing your antagonist's casual disregard for his fellow humans. This, more than anything else, will make your readers eager to see the antagonist defeated at the end of the novel.

SIX

The Stakes

Now you have your protagonist and antagonist clearly fixed in your novel. You know what motivates them. You know exactly what they want and how far they're willing to go to get it, meaning that the stakes of your novel should also be crystal clear. But are they clear to the reader? Do those stakes escalate through the novel to a satisfying climax? Having an intriguing character will bring your readers on board, but it's the stakes of the story that will keep them reading until the very last page. They already love your hero, but now they need to be worried about him, so they will continue reading to see if he accomplishes his goal or not.

. . .

What Does Your Protagonist Want?

When I'm editing, I often have a conversation with my writers where I ask them, "What does your hero *want*? Please, just tell me, because it's nowhere on the page that I can see." It's very common for writers to assume that readers will pick up on a hero's goals without being told, and they are hesitant to put it on the page.

I'm not sure why writers are so reluctant to state the hero's goal. We all grew up watching Disney movies, didn't we? Every single Disney heroine or hero has a goal, and they not only tell the audience what that goal is, they *sing* about it. The mermaid Ariel wants to be "part of that world." Simba the lion can't wait to be king. Moana is called to the sea, and sings about how far she'll go. Tiana sings about how she's "almost there" because she almost has enough money to open her own restaurant.

Writers for Disney call this the "I want that" song. They include it in every one of their movies because they know the audience needs to be told, flat-out, what the heroine wants. Most of you are writing for adults, not children. And you're writing novels, not musicals. Even so, you should be explicit about what your characters want. When you're revising, make sure you can point to the page or pages where the hero states his goal clearly, without any ambiguity. It's going to seem artificial and obvious at first, but readers want this information and they need to see it on the page in black and white.

In *Jaws* by Peter Benchley, Sheriff Brody has one goal. He wants to keep the people of Amity Island safe from the killer shark. He doesn't care about the loss of tourism dollars from closing the beach. He doesn't care about sucking up to the mayor so he can keep his job. He doesn't care about keeping the existence of the shark out of the newspapers. He wants to keep his people safe, full stop, and that goal is crystal clear to the reader.

In *To All the Boys I've Loved Before* by Jenny Han, the heroine, Lara Jean, has written five love letters to five boys, but has never sent them. The letters were just a way to put her feelings to rest. But her little sister finds the letters and mails them. Now the boy that Lara Jean truly loves knows the truth. The problem? He's her older sister's boyfriend. In order to convince him that it was only a childhood crush and she doesn't have feelings for him any longer, Lara Jean invents a fake relationship with the most popular guy in school. Her one goal is to not come between her sister and her sister's boyfriend. They must never find out her true feelings.

When her sister's boyfriend receives the letter and tries to talk to Lara Jean about it, she runs up to the school's most popular boy, throws her arms around him, and plants a huge kiss on his lips. The reader has no doubt that Lara Jean is serious about hiding her true feelings at any cost. We know this not only by what she thinks and what she says, but also by what she does.

When you're revising, make sure that you can point to the exact page where the heroine's goal is made clear to the reader. Make sure it's as straightforward as you can make it, so the reader knows exactly what the heroine wants.

How Important is This Goal?

Once you've clearly communicated the heroine's goal to the reader, make sure that goal or problem is so big that it takes a hundred percent of your heroine's time and attention. This should be the most important thing in her life right now. It's what she's spending her time on, it's the number one thing she's working for, and it's basically all she can think about.

The Big-Picture Revision Checklist

The reader cares about the heroine, but the heroine's problem is not the reader's problem. If the heroine dies, the reader will not die. If the heroine loses her job, the reader will not lose her job. Therefore, the reader is only capable of caring about the story problem a fraction of the amount the hero cares about it. If the hero cares one hundred percent, the reader might care seventy-five percent, or fifty percent.

What happens, then, if your hero is not all-in on this problem? What if the hero is willing to work at this problem up to a point, but no more than that?

Think about your favorite football team. Think about a game where they're losing, but they're bringing all of their heart and soul to the game. Every point they gain is hard-fought, but the team is pulling together, assisting each other, and the players on the sidelines are shouting encouragement to their teammates on the field. The stands are full of people dressed in team colors, cheering for every yard gained. When I watch a game like that, I'm on the edge of my seat.

But what happens when a football team is only phoning it in? Maybe it's an early-season game or an exhibition game. The team is still trying, but more for the paycheck than for the hope of winning. One player might score, but it's usually without much help from his teammates. If the cameras pan across the players on the sidelines, we see them clowning with each other, their eyes everywhere but the field. When I watch a game like that, my attention wanders, and I often turn it off at halftime, right around the time the stands are emptying.

You want your hero to be like the first example, not the second. Your hero's goal will be big, and at first it will seem unobtainable, especially in the face of such fierce opposition. There will be sacrifices along the way to solving this problem. Make sure that in your novel, the problem is so important to the hero that he will gladly make those sacrifices.

Dumplin' by Julie Murphy is about a plus-sized teenager named Willowdean, who is the daughter of a former beauty queen. Willowdean decides to enter the Miss Teen Bluebonnet Pageant—the very pageant that her mom now runs. At first, Willowdean is only in it to poke fun at shallow and artificial beauty standards. But the deeper she gets into pageant culture, the more she wants to win, not just for herself, but for plus-sized girls everywhere. Phoning it in for laughs was one thing, but seriously competing in a beauty pageant is nearly a fulltime job. There are dance rehearsals, costume fittings,

The Big-Picture Revision Checklist

hair and makeup appointments, and Willowdean needs to develop a talent. Ethically, her mom can't help her with any of it, and since Willowdean has never competed before, she has to work harder and longer than any of the other girls in order to have a shot. She puts a tremendous amount of time and effort into learning how to be a beauty queen, never letting herself relax or take a day off, and readers cheer her commitment.

In *The Lord of the Rings* by J.R.R. Tolkien, Frodo is on an epic quest. He's walking across the kingdom carrying a cursed ring that is slowly sapping his will. He has to throw the ring into Mount Doom before succumbing to its power, or the entire kingdom will fall. Frodo will do whatever it takes to bring the ring to Mount Doom. He and his allies are fighting as hard as possible to make that happen. They will travel far from home, go wherever they have to go, fight whoever they have to fight to make it happen. Frodo is dogged in his quest. He rests as little as possible, often doesn't stop to eat, and doesn't take time to bathe or clean himself. He is single-minded in his push forward. And because Frodo wants it so badly, the reader wants it too. Every mile closer Frodo gets to Mount Doom, the more we want this to happen for him and for Middle Earth, and we're devastated by every setback Frodo suffers.

What If Your Protagonist Fails?

Your heroine's goal must have two sides to it. There is the prize to be won if she succeeds, but there also must be consequences for failure. If the heroine can fail at this goal, and then go back to her normal life no worse for wear, then you have some revising to do. Make it so that failure is not an option. The heroine *can't* go back to her normal life after this. If she fails, everything will be worse than when the story began.

There should be a time limit to what your heroine is after. If she has all the time in the world to accomplish her goal, then there isn't any consequence for failure. She can simply try again, and again. Make sure this is your heroine's *one* chance to fix this problem or achieve this goal.

For example, let's pretend that you're writing a YA novel where the heroine must bring up her grades in order to get into college. If she's in her first semester of tenth grade, then she's got plenty of time and several chances to turn those Ds into As. However, what if your heroine is in her senior year and has been provisionally accepted to a community college, provided she bring her grades up in the final semester? Now everything is on the line. Add in a difficult teacher who won't give her a break, a lab partner who sabotages her chemistry experiments, and a desperately-needed part time job that cuts into homework time, and now you've got real stakes.

When you're revising, ask yourself, how can I make the consequences worse? Can I make them life or death? Please say yes, because the stakes in every successful novel must be nothing short of life or death.

Sometimes this means literal death is at stake, such as in *The Hunger Games* and *Jaws*. In most thrillers and fantasy novels, the stakes are just that obvious. The hero wins or he dies. However, the life-or-death stakes in your novel don't have to be literal. But there does have to be symbolic life or death. Failure for your hero means death *of some kind*. Death of a career. Death of a relationship. Death of freedom. Death of social standing. Even death of a sense of self. No matter the stakes, failure should feel like a kind of death to your hero.

In *The Princess Bride* by William Goldman, the stakes are true love. In act one, Westley leaves to seek his fortune, and Buttercup thinks he's been killed by pirates. She says, "I will never love again." Westley was her one true love, and his death is the death of any hope for happiness for Buttercup. Later, when Westley turns up very much alive, every choice Buttercup makes and every risk she takes is so she won't lose him again. She's even willing to be separated from him for a short time if it means he will live. It's her only hope of ever being happy.

In the same novel, Inigo Montoya is on a quest to avenge his father's death. He's been training for twenty years to achieve this goal, and almost fails at it when Count Rugen stabs him during their sword fight. Inigo is not at all worried that Count Rugen will kill him. He's only worried that he will fail his father. That is the true consequence. Failing his father will feel like death to Inigo. Against that prospect, his actual death isn't even that important.

In the novel *Where'd You Go, Bernadette?* by Maria Semple, Bernadette has a sagging career and no friends. She hates where she lives, and she's pulling away from her family. She feels like she's disappearing. Until one day, she really does disappear. She has run away to find out who she really is. That's her big problem to solve. The life-or-death stakes are Bernadette's sense of self.

As you're revising, think about a failure that will feel like death to your heroine. Or perhaps even worse than death. That's what needs to be at stake in your story.

Forward!

Let me tell you something about humans. It's very hard to get someone to change direction in their life. Moving toward a goal is extremely hard and most people won't stick with things long enough to make lasting change. (Hello, broken New Year resolutions!) People are scared. People are lazy. If someone can quit with few or no consequences? He'll quit. It's much easier to justify the status quo than to shake it up.

Fictional characters are the same way. So as the author, you need to be very mean to your imaginary friends. You need to set up the plot in such a way that the heroine can't go back. She can only go forward. Be sure that you're not so caught up in your plot that you lose sight of the bigger picture. As the author, you know where you want your heroine to end up, so you push her toward that goal, forgetting that there is an easy out that any reasonable human would take. Of course, your heroine is determined and she wants this big goal, but you'll still have to force her into it by closing all the doors behind her.

In *The Hunger Games* by Suzanne Collins, once Katniss raises her hand and says, "I volunteer as tribute!" she is on a one-way ticket to the Hunger Games. She gets a new dress. She gets put on TV. They put her on a train and send her to the capitol. Even if she changed her mind at that point, tough luck. She needs to see this all the way through to the end. She's either going to win the Hunger Games or die trying.

In *The Underground Railroad* by Colson Whitehead, Cora is an enslaved person on a plantation in Georgia. After planning and thinking it over, Cora and two companions make their escape one night. First, they travel on foot, and are later helped by others to run faster and farther by wagon and then by train. Cora relishes every bit of freedom she finds, but what's constantly on her mind is what would happen to her if she were ever caught and returned to the plantation. She's seen the public torture that enslaved people are subjected to when they are recaptured. Once she sets a single foot off the plantation, she is on a one-way journey, since a fate worse than death awaits her if she turns back. She has no choice but to keep going.

Even if death isn't on the line, make sure that you haven't given your hero an easy way out. Because if there is one, the reader will wonder why the hero didn't take it. In *The Hundred Foot Journey* by Richard C. Morais, the Haji family has sunk their life's savings into their new restaurant, and they have to make a go of it because they can't afford to start over somewhere else. In *The Wizard of Oz* by L. Frank Baum, Dorothy has to take the yellow brick road all the way to the Emerald City if she has any hope of making it home to Kansas.

Taking that first step into a new adventure was your hero's choice, but once he's made that choice, it must be irrevocable. In fiction, there are no backsies. Win or lose, he's got to see it through to the end.

It's Personal

The stakes in your story should matter. But is bigger always better? Authors have been told over and over to "raise the stakes." However, many authors think it means they have to keep piling on bigger and bigger consequences. It's not enough for the house to be haunted. The whole neighborhood has to be haunted. The whole town. Maybe the whole state! It's not enough for the hero to be running for his life. He should be trying to save his family too. He has to save the city. He has to save the whole world!

But the paradox is that the bigger we try to make the stakes, the less readers are invested in them. You can't actually raise the stakes by making them *bigger*. Human brains don't work that way. When presented with suffering on a mass scale, we become numb.

You don't raise the stakes by making them bigger. You raise the stakes by making them *matter more*. How do you do that? You make them more personal.

In *The Hitchhiker's Guide to the Galaxy* by Douglas Adams, the planet Earth is obliterated at the first plot point, and readers aren't worried. This is as big as big stakes could be, and yet, readers are unmoved. In fact, Douglas Adams plays it for laughs. However, a few pages later, our hero and his best friend are about to be shoved out a spaceship's airlock and readers turn the pages faster and faster, hoping they will be okay. The difference? The destruction of the Earth was too big, and our worry too diffuse, with nothing concrete to focus on. But two lovable guys with no weapons or other resources about to be put to death for no reason other than being in the wrong place at the wrong time? It's terrible! We must read on!

Some genres have personal stakes built in. Maybe you're writing women's fiction where the stakes are the heroine finally understanding her mother. Maybe you're writing romance where the stakes are a couple's true love. Maybe you're writing a middle-grade novel where the stakes are the hero standing up to the popular kids and embracing his true nerdiness. It's awesome when the stakes are on that personal level, because when readers connect with the characters, they will care intensely about the outcome of the story.

However, other genres rely on more general, global stakes. Lots of fantasy novels have the fate of the kingdom at stake. Many thrillers have the fate of the whole world hanging in the balance. But even when you're writing a big, epic book filled with world-ending consequences, you still have to find a way to make those stakes personal. Who is the hero truly trying to save? Himself? His sister? His parents? His lover? The only way that stakes matter to readers is if they're brought down from the global to the human level. Do whatever you can to bring it to a personal level and tell us why the fate of the whole world matters to this hero and his friends.

The Lord of the Rings by J.R.R. Tolkien is a huge trilogy with a huge cast and a plot that takes us all over Middle Earth. But what we remember from that book is one little hobbit who had to carry one small ring. And Frodo was willing to go far from home, and fight as hard as he did, not for the whole kingdom, but for the people who were counting on him. For his friends. For Sam and Merry and Pippin and Aragorn. And most especially for the people of the shire—his little village. Home. That is who Frodo was fighting for. He was fighting for his family and friends, because that's who he cared about. And because Frodo cared so much, the readers did too.

The novel *Good Omens* by Terry Pratchett and Neil Gaiman is about a centuries-long friendship between an angel and a demon. When the Antichrist is unleashed and it's about to be Armageddon, the angel and the demon have to team up to save the world. Heaven doesn't want it saved. Hell doesn't want it saved. But these two guys do. Desperately. They want to save the world so their friendship can go on. The fate of the whole world *is* personal to them.

You absolutely should have stakes as big as the world if that's what your genre demands. Readers love to see you blow things up and put cities in peril and worry that the world will end. But make sure that you've also made these things matter to one person, to a group of heroes, or to one small hobbit who just wants to make it home for second breakfast.

SEVEN

The Five Big Scenes

When you're doing your big-picture revising, it's best to save the plot for last. Getting clear on a protagonist's motivations, making an antagonist more powerful, and making the stakes matter more often leads to changes in the plot. And that's okay. Plots are more flexible than most writers think. Often, when writers are working on their first drafts, they're only thinking in terms of *this happens* and then *that happens.* They're thinking about events, not story. However, when the first draft is done, the writer has a chance to step back and look at the novel as a whole, and that often means that the plot is something different than the one a writer started out with. Stories can go in wild directions, with many twists along the way, as long as the framework is solid and the stakes keep escalating.

All the foundational work you did in the previous chapters will make your plot easier to revise. For example, making sure the protagonist is likable will help with the hook. And knowing what's at stake means knowing how to write the climax.

A novel is a big thing. It's too big to hold in your head. There's no way a writer can concentrate on every scene, every chapter, and every detail at once. But what a writer can do is consider the overall flow of the book. Humans have been telling stories the same way forever. We introduce a character and her world, add complications and setbacks in the middle, and come to a resolution at the end, answering the big story question and showing how the heroine has changed. This is the universal storytelling template.

If your story structure is basically sound, readers will forgive other sins like awkward dialogue, stilted description, or overused metaphors. However, if the story structure is wobbly, or your biggest scenes are falling flat, readers will quickly lose interest.

. . .

Structure is Important

There isn't a "formula" for a good plot, but there is a broad basic pattern that is common to all stories. You should think of your novel in three acts, with big turning points at the break into each act, as well as a high point in the middle of act two. Start with the hook, which intrigues a reader. At about twenty percent (or earlier in faster-paced novels), there is a change which propels the heroine on the story journey. There's a big scene right at midpoint filled with action, drama, and emotion. At about the three-quarter mark, the heroine is brought low and nearly gives up. But she rises strong for the final showdown of the climax.

When we revise for plot, the place to start is with these five biggest scenes: the hook, plot point one, the midpoint, the all-is-lost moment, and the climax. These are the big turning points in your novel, where the plot goes in a new direction. These are the scenes that readers will remember the most. Therefore, it's crucial to nail these big scenes first, because they will form the foundation of the novel. The rest of the scenes are built around them.

First, are these five big scenes even *there*? Take out a copy of your manuscript. Can you point to the scene where act one ends and act two begins?

The Big-Picture Revision Checklist

When you open your manuscript to the exact middle, is there a scene that marks a major turning point?

It sounds like a silly question, but when I'm editing, I often can't find that first big turning point. Characters simply drift into their story adventure without quite knowing how they got there. Other writers skip the all-is-lost scene. It's too painful to write, and authors don't want to hurt their beloved characters, so they don't let them fall too far before pulling them back to victory. Some writers never write a strong midpoint scene, and then struggle with a middle section that drags.

Once you've determined that these big scenes are present and in the right order, it's time to look at them one by one. Every scene in your novel should push the narrative forward. Every scene should be filled with emotion and character change. But these five big scenes have additional jobs to do. So start here. Fixing other scenes should come later, after you get the top five right. And once you've made these five big scenes as good as you can make them, all the scenes surrounding them will be much easier to revise.

. . .

The Hook

The hook is the opening scene of your novel. Its job is to introduce the hero, introduce the story world, and draw the reader in. That's it. Some authors want to get the plot cooking right on page one, and that's fine if you can do it, but it's not as crucial as establishing the story world and the character. In your hook, if you have to choose between establishing character and starting the plot, choose character.

However, this doesn't mean starting with backstory or static description. You must hook your reader by showing an interesting person doing interesting things. That means a *scene*. Not flat description, not backstory, not explanations of how we got here, not memory or reminiscing. A scene. That means action, dialogue, your heroine's thoughts and emotions, and all five senses should be present on the page in a scene that is moving the action forward—even if it's just a little bit forward. You don't have a lot of time to hook a reader, so you'll have to introduce a person and a place with just a few punchy details rather than long paragraphs of description.

It's through this scene that readers will understand who the heroine is and where the story takes place. It's these two factors that will determine whether or not they wish to spend their time reading your book. Readers sample a tiny excerpt—just a few pages—before deciding to buy a novel. If you start with backstory or description, or concentrate on explaining the world to the readers, they will stop reading. They may not be able to say exactly why they put down your book, but they will instinctively know that they're not interested enough because you haven't given them someone to root for or any hints about problems to come.

The Martian by Andy Weir is about an astronaut who is stranded alone on Mars and needs to survive long enough to get rescued. The novel opens at the moment when astronaut Mark Watney regains consciousness and realizes three things: he's badly wounded, his crew has left him, and if he doesn't get to shelter immediately, he's going to die. He starts assessing the situation and figures out what he can do right now, right this minute, to survive.

It's an effective opening chapter because the reader is introduced to the story world and to the hero. We see Mark in action, making his way to shelter while dealing with the harsh Mars atmosphere. In chapter one, the reader knows they are with a hero who is smart and determined, on an unforgiving planet, and there is trouble ahead. All this is on the page without the burden of backstory or exposition. Do we know how and why he got into this situation? Nope.

Later, in chapters two and three and four, we find out how Mark Watney got to Mars and why his crew left him. But for chapter one, all we need to know is that there is a likable guy in trouble, and we will read on to see how he survives Mars.

The Lightning Thief by Rick Riordan has one of the best opening hooks I've ever seen. In fact, the entire novel hits its story beats like clockwork, so it's an excellent case study for anyone who is trying to learn story structure. But I especially love the hook.

Percy Jackson is a middle school kid who is at a horrible boarding school, and today, his class is taking a field trip to the museum. On the way, one of his teachers makes a point of giving Percy a special pen. At the museum, another teacher turns into a harpy and tries to kill him. Percy's pen turns into a magical sword, which he uses to defeat the harpy.

It's a scene full of action that also tells the reader exactly who Percy Jackson is. He's a lonely middle school kid with unique and awesome abilities in a world where some adults are trying to kill him while others try to help. In chapter one, the reader has no idea why Percy is at a horrible boarding school, or why someone would try to kill him, or how he has the power to vanquish magical creatures. The reader doesn't *want* to know. Not yet. The explanations come in the next two chapters, and readers are willing to wait. All the reader wants from an opening chapter is enough information to decide to read on, delivered in the form of a scene. *The Lightning Thief* gives us an intriguing character, an interesting world, and exciting action. Is it any wonder that the book was a hit with kids and the start of a bestselling series?

But a hook doesn't have to have sword fights or spaceships in order to intrigue a reader. *A Gentleman in Moscow* by Amor Towles begins with hardly any action at all. It's 1922 and Count Alexander Rostov has been sentenced to house arrest at the hotel where he lives, right across from the Kremlin. Two soldiers escort him home, while the bellman moves his belongings from the luxury suite he'd been living in to maid's quarters in the attic. Through it all, Rostov retains his good humor. He jokes with the hotel staff and the soldiers, seemingly unbothered by his fall from grace, refusing to let anyone see him crack. He pretends he's on an ocean voyage, discovers that his bedsprings squeak in the key of G-sharp, and greets the pigeons nesting near his window like old friends. Nothing really happens beyond unpacking, yet readers are eager to read on, because the author has given us a delightful character in an interesting place. Readers want to know two things—how did Rostov get into this mess, and how will he adapt to his new life?

As you're revising, take a look at your opening chapter. Will readers know who your heroine is— not by what she thinks or what she says, but by what she *does*? Have you given your reader a glimpse into your story world? Have things started to move forward? Is there enough conflict to make readers want to know what happens next, or at least an intriguing story question to be answered? Have you saved the explanations and backstory for later chapters?

Plot Point One

After your hook is as good as you can make it, take a look at plot point one. This is also called the break into (act) two, crossing the first threshold, the leap of faith, or the doorway of no return. It's a point that comes about twenty percent into the book, (sometimes sooner in fast-paced books) and it's what truly starts the heroine on her journey. In the Hero's Journey template, this is when the hero answers the call to adventure and crosses from the ordinary world into the new world of the story.

There are two keys to making sure that plot point one works in your novel. First, there has to be a definitive break from the world where the heroine began into the new world of the story. Think of *The Wizard of Oz* movie going from black and white to technicolor. It doesn't have to be as dramatic as that, but there has to be something new that takes the heroine out of her old life into a new one. A new job, a new school, a new location, a new baby, new love interest, or new plot complications that change everything. In a thriller, this might be the first time someone tries to kill the hero, and what he decides to do about it. In romance, it's when the hero and heroine meet, and decide to pursue their attraction.

The second key is that whatever happens at plot point one has to be under the protagonist's control. In *The Hobbit* by J.R.R. Tolkien, this is the moment when Bilbo agrees to help the dwarves retrieve their treasure. In *The Wonderful Wizard of Oz* by L. Frank Baum, this is the moment when Dorothy says yes, I will walk the yellow brick road to the Emerald City. In *The Devil Wears Prada* by Lauren Weisberger, it's the moment that Andi takes the job working for *Runway*. In *Jurassic Park*, it's the moment when Alan Grant says yes, I will go visit your dinosaur park for the weekend.

Some authors miss the chance to nail plot point one because they think this plot point is all about what happens to the hero, rather than what he decides to do about it. There will be events outside the hero's control that will force him to make a decision here, but his choice is the most important thing. Bilbo had no control over whether or not he was invited to go on this quest. The offer came to him. Dorothy had no control over the tornado that lifted her house and dropped it in Oz. Andi didn't control whether she'd get the job offer at *Runway*.

However, what the heroes decide to do *next* is the key to making plot point one sing. Bilbo chooses to go on an adventure. Dorothy decides to follow the yellow brick road, which leads her even farther from home. Andi takes the job.

When you're revising, make sure that at your first plot point, your heroine is the one making the decision that leads her to the heart of the story.

. . .

Midpoint

The next scene to look at is your midpoint scene. What happens exactly halfway through your book that sends the plot in a new direction? In *Jurassic Park* by Michael Crichton, hungry carnivorous dinosaurs have escaped from their cages, and they're on the hunt. In *The Wonderful Wizard of Oz* by L. Frank Baum, Dorothy gets to the Emerald City, only to discover that she can't get home without stealing the witch's broomstick. The plot is moving in a completely different direction now.

The midpoint scene is where character and plot collide. Up to now, the hero has been using his usual coping methods to deal with new problems. He's been fumbling a lot, but mostly muddling through. At the midpoint, there is a reversal of fortune, as the hero's first big attempt to solve the story problem fails. In many cases, secrets are revealed or new information is brought to light, and the hero discovers that the problem he *thought* he was solving is much worse than he ever thought possible.

In *Sense and Sensibility* by Jane Austen, the midpoint is where both Dashwood sisters discover that they're being wooed under false pretenses. Elinor's been spending a lot of time with Edward, but he's secretly engaged to another woman. Marianne's boyfriend won't marry her because she's not rich. These revelations send the romance plots careening in a new direction. Marianne can't ever be rich enough to satisfy Willoughby. Elinor realizes that Edward will never see her as more than a friend.

In *The Hitchhiker's Guide to the Galaxy* by Douglas Adams, Arthur Dent has survived the destruction of planet Earth by hitching a ride on a passing spaceship. That spaceship is owned by hostile aliens, who eject Arthur and his guide, Ford Prefect, out the airlock and into space. At that exact moment, another spaceship picks them up. This midpoint scene is filled with improbable coincidences, because the person who picked them up is Ford's old friend, who is traveling with the girl that Arthur tried to date, and they are in a stolen spaceship that they don't quite know how to operate. The characters soon realize that the ship is powered by an "improbability drive," which passes through every point in the universe at the same time, and improbable coincidences are going to keep happening as long as they are traveling on this ship.

The Hitchhiker's Guide to the Galaxy is a silly and fun book, but even within its wacky plot, you can see the bones of good structure. In the opening pages, Arthur Dent is introduced, and the focus is on his character. Arthur is an everyman, a bit naive, but good-natured and earnest. At plot point one, he escapes Earth moments before it explodes, casting him into the extraordinary world of an outer space hitchhiker. At the midpoint, everything changes, as Arthur realizes that the universe is much larger—and much stranger—than anyone ever thought possible, and his escape from Earth was just the beginning of a quest for the very meaning of existence.

When you're revising, open your manuscript to the exact center. What's happening on that page, or pages close to it? You should be seeing a scene filled with action, emotion, and drama. Action, because things are happening. Emotion, because the characters care deeply about it. And drama, because this new direction for the plot complicates everything.

All is Lost

Roughly three-quarters of the way through a novel comes a moment where things seem bleak. The heroine thinks she's failed. She almost gives up because she feels defeated. This moment is called the all-is-lost moment. It's also sometimes called the dark night of the soul or plot point two. This is the moment when things are as bad as they can get.

Some writers skip over this moment, or give it a scant paragraph or two and then move on. Writers are often uncomfortable with these hopeless emotions and want to spare their heroes. When you love your characters a lot, you don't like to cause them pain.

But you should make this moment matter. Spend time on it. Let your hero really *feel* those awful feelings. Let him wallow a bit. Make him feel defeated on every level. Not only did your hero fail, but the failure was in some ways his own fault.

In the last quarter of the novel, when the hero picks himself up and dusts himself off and gives it one last try, the victory will be all the sweeter. Without that low point, the climax doesn't matter as much. So dig deep here, and get all up in your feelings. Then put those feelings on the page.

In the novel *The Devil Wears Prada* by Lauren Weisberger, Andi is working for the boss from hell, who is the editor of a fashion magazine. At the all-is-lost moment, Andi tells off her boss in front of basically the entire fashion world. She screams at Miranda during a runway show, including a well-placed f-bomb, and that's the end of Andi's job. She thinks it's also the end of her life in New York and the end of her career in publishing. Andi spends a lot of time wallowing in her sorrow before she gets her life back together.

In *Dork Diaries*, a middle-grade novel by Rachel Renée Russell, Nikki is a scholarship student at a private school who has a locker next to the richest, most popular, most beautiful, and meanest girl in the school. MacKenzie has every advantage over Nikki, and humiliates her at every turn, making her a social outcast. Nikki has a glimmer of hope that her artistic talent will improve her social life, since talent is the one thing that MacKenzie can't buy. Nikki enters her finest painting in the school art show, but the day of the show, Nikki's dad accidentally runs over the painting while dropping her off at school, right in front of MacKenzie, who points and laughs and flounces into the school carrying her perfect artwork.

What can Nikki do but sit on the curb next to her ruined painting and cry? This is Nikki's breaking point. She's tried and tried to fit in at this snobby school and she can't take it anymore. She decides to drop out and go back to public school.

When you're revising, make sure your all-is-lost

moment feels like a true defeat. She's reached absolute bottom. The heroine has lost and *knows* she's lost. This is only temporary, and things will change in the final quarter of the book, but for now, make sure your heroine thinks that all is truly lost—and make sure your reader thinks so too.

The Climax

Finally, ask yourself if your climax scene is as strong as it can be. Are all the essential people on the page? Does your heroine have a central role? Is she ready to finally deal with the problem before her? Is this the scene that's going to decide the outcome once and for all?

A climax has two jobs. First, it must resolve the central story problem for good. Whatever problem your heroine has been struggling with for the whole novel ends now. Either she achieves this goal or she doesn't, and this is a fight she's never going to fight again. The second thing a climax must do is show the specific ways in which the heroine has changed. Because of everything the plot has put her through, she's a better person, and one who is more than capable of taking on the antagonist.

In some genres, your heroine has trained for a

physical fight—one she can now win. In other genres, she's become more compassionate, with new understanding that allows her to reconcile with the antagonist. Dealing with an antagonist isn't one-size-fits-all. Make sure you're giving the readers the kind of ending they expect from your genre.

If you're writing mystery, thriller, science fiction, fantasy, or horror, your novel should end with the defeat of the antagonist. That might be death, it might be prison, it might be banishment. Whatever it takes for the reader to understand that the antagonist's days of causing trouble are over. The heroine has leveled-up to a point where she's strong enough to defeat the antagonist once and for all.

However, in most literary fiction, YA, coming of age novels, and romance, the novel ends with reconciliation. The heroine has changed, and she's changed in the specific way she needed to in order for this reconciliation to happen. She's come to a new understanding or acceptance and can now make peace with the person who has been making her nuts for most of the novel.

In *The Lion, The Witch and the Wardrobe* by C.S. Lewis, everything in the novel points to that final confrontation. There are the forces of good—the four Pevensie children and their magical talking lion, and there are the forces of evil—the White Witch and her allies. It's an epic battle. All of Narnia is involved and there is archery and sword fighting and people riding polar bears. It's not going to end until one side is utterly defeated.

But your novel doesn't have to have magical creatures and hand-to-hand combat in order to be epic. If you're writing a coming of age novel, the climax will be something that shows the new maturity of the hero. Most literary fiction and women's fiction ends with reconciliation or a new understanding. Romance ends with a kiss. *Sense and Sensibility* by Jane Austen ends with grand declarations of love and a double wedding. In *Dumplin'* by Julie Murphy, the beauty pageant is a vehicle for Willowdean and her mother to make peace with one another, as they each finally understand where the other is coming from.

When you're revising, think about your genre, and what readers of that genre expect from a climax. What is your genre's version of an epic ending? Have you done that? Has your hero changed in such a way that makes this ending possible?

. . .

All the Rest

Once you have the five biggest scenes in place, and they are doing the job they are supposed to, with all the action, emotion, and drama, then the other scenes in your novel will be much easier to revise. You *will* have to revise every scene, not only those on this checklist, but now you'll know how, because you'll have these big turning points as beacons.

These five scenes are the highlight reel of your novel. Once you've got these five scenes perfected, you'll have a much clearer handle on how to revise the other scenes in your novel. The scenes before them will be the buildup. The scenes following them will detail the fallout or the resolution from them. So start here, and make sure you nail these scenes first.

EIGHT

Beta Readers

You've been writing and revising your book alone, and you've taken it as far as you can by yourself. Perhaps you've gone through the checklist and changed a few chapters. Maybe you sharpened characters and streamlined your plot. Perhaps you've made so many changes that you've lost sight of the big picture. Maybe you're asking yourself, does this novel even work anymore? Have I actually improved things? Did I cut too much? Did I add too much? Did changing some scenes mean that others no longer work?

It's common at this point to have read through a novel so many times that you're not sure what, exactly, is on the page. You think you've got a solid story, but what's in your head might not be what other people see. The only way to break through this is to get an outside perspective. It's time to show your novel to other people. But don't show it to the whole world. Not yet. The first people to see your novel should be your trusted circle of beta readers.

What is a Beta Reader?

The term comes from the software industry. Beta testers test new software, running it through its paces to find all the bugs before it's shipped for sale. In the same way, a beta reader is a friend who will read your manuscript and tell you what needs fixing. A beta will point out inconsistencies and plot holes, tell you what's confusing, or when the pace drags. They will also tell you what you're doing right.

This is different from the services of a paid editor. This is a volunteer job. It's a beautiful gift that writers and friends of writers give one another. Beta readers don't have to be writers themselves, although it helps. More importantly, they have to be good readers who you trust to give you honest feedback.

. . .

How do You Find Them?

The number one question I get asked in my writing classes is, "How do I find a beta reader?" I get it. Everyone is desperate for feedback, and it's hard to imagine you can just hand your manuscript to someone and they will happily read it and give you their honest opinion. It seems almost too good to be true. But honestly, it's not hard to find beta readers.

Start with your own social circle. You probably have at least one aspiring writer among your friends. If not, it's time to make more friends. I'm serious about this. Find your people! A writer's career is enhanced greatly by having a tribe of other writers to pal around with. We exchange career advice, book recommendations, and writing tips. There is nothing like the support of your fellow writers. Look for other writers at critique groups hosted by bookstores, libraries, or community centers. Go to writing conferences or genre conferences near you. Join NaNoWriMo (National Novel Writing Month) and attend the write-ins that they sponsor. If you can't find a local writing group, form one.

So how do you go from friend-who-writes to trusted beta? Let me give you a script to follow. The next time you're talking to your friend about writing, say to her, "Hey, if you ever need a beta read, hit me up." That's it. That's the entire script.

Usually, your friend will say, "Yes, and I'd be happy to read for you too." But even if she doesn't say that, it's okay. You've introduced the subject, and I promise your friend will not forget. Everyone is desperate for beta readers and if you offer, someone will accept.

Notice that I'm talking about *giving* beta reads. That's how it starts. You often have to give critiques before you receive one. It's good for you to read and critique other people's manuscripts. You'll learn from every critique you give. And if you give beta reads promptly, with honesty and good intentions, that karma will come back to you.

Respect Your Betas

Someone reading and critiquing your manuscript is doing you a huge favor. It's hard work and it takes a lot of time. You don't have to pay your beta, or buy them a gift, or give them anything beyond your thanks, but it's vital that you give them your respect. You show that respect in three ways.

First, give your beta reader as close to a finished

manuscript as you possibly can. Many writers are so eager for feedback that they rush the manuscript to their betas. If your manuscript is out with your beta reader, but you're still revising it, then you've given it to your beta too soon. You need to revise your novel to the best of your ability, proofread it, and then give it to your beta. Take the book as far as you possibly can on your own before getting input from others.

Also, give your beta reader the manuscript in whatever format she prefers. Some betas only want to read hard copy. Some want a Microsoft Word document. Some want a fully-formatted book they can read on an e-reader. The format is not up to the writer, it's up to the reader. You also have to take feedback in whatever form your beta reader gives you. Some write in the margins. Some write all of their comments on a separate document. Some do both. If your beta reader asks you how you like your feedback, you can give suggestions, but most beta readers will do what they want to do, and you have to accept that.

Second, thank your beta readers. Even if you disagree with every single thing your beta reader said, you still owe them thanks. They gave you something priceless—their time. I used to beta read regularly for a close friend, until he started taking my critiques for granted. One time, he didn't even thank me. I don't beta read for him anymore.

You should not discuss any specific suggestions with your beta. If you do, you're putting your beta reader on the spot, making her think she has to justify her critique. You can apply or discard any of the comments you wish, but privately. In public, to your reader's face, you *loved* all of her critique and you found it *so helpful*. I often write my thank-you email to my beta reader before I even glance at her critique. I gush about how much I loved it and how the manuscript will be improved by her comments, and how eager I am to go back to the novel and improve it thanks to her help. *Then* I read her critique.

Third, never argue with a beta reader. Never, ever do that. You will never agree one hundred percent with a critique—nor should you. Your beta won't know which part of their critique you used and which you didn't, nor will they care. Always value the friendship over a beta read. If you don't agree with one single thing your beta says, that's okay. If they hate your novel, that's okay too. Dump the critique and keep the friendship, not vice-versa.

. . .

Incorporating Feedback

Let a critique sink in for a day before acting on it. Emotions get hot when reading a critique of your own work. If they didn't, you wouldn't be human. Everyone, from new writer to old pro, needs to let things cool before starting in on a rewrite. A day later, things will look very different.

You'll need to sort the feedback into one of four types. The first two are easily dealt with. If your beta pointed out an easy-to-fix mistake, such as a factual error or poor word choice, you simply correct it and move on. Sometimes your beta has some wacky out-of-left field remark that has more to do with him than with you. For example, let's say your beta just broke up with his blond girlfriend and therefore he hates the fact that your heroine is blond. Ignore that.

The third kind of feedback is more labor intensive. Betas have an uncanny knack for pointing out problems that you kind of knew were there, but didn't want to admit to yourself. Perhaps you hoped you could get away with leaving them in the manuscript. Perhaps you hoped no one would notice the problems because the rest of the manuscript was strong. Betas *always* notice. If your beta reader pointed out problems with something huge like pacing or characterization or a giant plot hole, you might agree with the feedback but feel overwhelmed at how much work it will take to fix. Don't despair. Go back to the revision checklist and follow the steps, and soon you'll be back on track.

The fourth kind of feedback you'll get is the kind where your beta reader wants to solve the problem for you. This can derail you if you're not careful. Often, a beta reader will tell you how *she* would fix your manuscript, which isn't how *you* should fix it. "That Bob character? He's great, but having him be a circus clown doesn't really fit your murder mystery. It would be far better for Bob to be a police officer, don't you think?" Nope, probably not.

However, you can't just dismiss feedback like this. You can't say, "No cops!" and be done. You still have to address the *problem* even if the *solution* isn't correct. You'll have to ask yourself why the circus clown character doesn't work. Have you made Bob a shy introvert? That doesn't fit with a clown. Have you made Bob a morning person? Hard to do that when the circus performs at night. So you might want to change Bob's character to fit a circus clown. You might want to make him an extroverted night owl. But most likely, the solution is a third thing. If you're writing a murder mystery at the circus, maybe your main character isn't a clown at all. Maybe Bob is the circus financial manager, who is a shy person, counting receipts and doing his books first thing in the morning.

Most of the time, this third solution is better than the original and also better than what your beta came up with. A clown doesn't work and neither does a police officer, but a circus manager does. In order to get to that better place, you have to approach a critique with an open mind and an ability to read between the lines. Always fix problems your way, but *do* fix them.

It's up to you how much of a critique you want to take in. Your beta gave you free advice, and you can choose to use it or not. Beta readers know that you'll only take a fraction of what they propose. You are never under any obligation to report back to your beta about which part of her critique you used. That is not part of the deal. So revise with abandon, taking exactly what you need from a critique and no more.

Be kind to yourself during this process. No matter how much you crave that feedback, it's going to sting. It gets easier the more you do it, but it's always hard to hear that your novel isn't perfect yet.

You thought you were done. You thought your manuscript was perfect, and now you see that it's not, and you still have a lot of work to do. Don't beat yourself up. In fact, you should be proud! It might feel like you've taken a huge step backward, but you're actually far ahead of where you were before you got feedback.

Pay it Back (Or Forward)

Finally, remember that your beta reader has done you a great favor, so find a way to pay it back. If your beta is also a writer, offer to read and critique a manuscript of hers in the future. If your beta reader is not a writer, then pay it forward by offering to read another writer's work. Giving beta reads is how you pay your dues as part of the writing community. And it's just good karma. You will learn from every beta read you give, you'll gain confidence in your writing abilities, and you'll earn the positive regard of your fellow writers. It's a win all the way around.

NINE

Getting to the Finish Line

How do you know when you're finished editing? How much is enough? I have read books—bestselling books—that I, personally, think could use more editing. I'm sure you have too. On the flipside, we all know people who have been revising the same novel for five years or even ten years, and they just can't ever seem to finish. Why? Because editing is a trap.

Editing is a Trap

You know those action movies where the hero's girlfriend or wife or sister is kidnapped? We've all seen these movies and we all know how they go. The bad guy calls the hero and says, "I've got your loved one. Meet me down at the shipping docks at midnight. Don't call the cops or she's dead." And what does the hero's best friend say? "Don't go! It's a trap." The hero always looks very earnest and tortured while he packs up his guns. He turns to his friend and says, "I know it's a trap, but I have to go anyway."

Editing is like that. It's a trap, *but you have to go anyway.*

What I mean is, you *do* have to edit. That's a given. But once you start, it's hard to stop. You can always make things better. You can always punch up a line of dialogue, or make a descriptive passage a bit more evocative, or add a tiny section to your characterization. That's the trap. The danger is that someone will keep revising the same novel forever.

When I was editing for a small press, I once had an author who couldn't let his book go even though he had a publishing contract. I did multiple rounds of edits with him, giving him positive feedback and encouragement all the while. Even when I assured him that he was done revising and he could turn the book over for copyedits, he still wanted to make changes. He held the manuscript back, and missed the deadline to turn it in. Then he missed the extension. And the extension after that. A year later, the press canceled his book.

Many authors have projects like that. They keep fiddling and fiddling, sure that just one more pass will finally make it perfect. But after a year or two (or five) on the same manuscript, you aren't really improving the work. You're not making it better, you're just making it different. At that point, you're just artfully managing your fear. Because if you never finish, you never have to send it out. You never have to face rejection or critical judgement. You're free to tinker forever, without the terrifying prospect of actually letting the public see your work.

More importantly, spending years polishing one book means you're not improving *as a writer*. If you're not moving on to new work, you're not learning new skills and you're not growing. Endlessly polishing one single book is the most self-defeating thing you can do.

Your task as a writer is not to write one perfect book. It's to write many books. That's what writers do.

If you're caught in the trap, take a breath, give yourself a hard deadline, and stick to it. Tell yourself that two weeks from now, or a month from now, or before the new year, you're going to stop revising. When the deadline comes, put the current book away and start something new. You don't have to send the book out to agents and editors. You don't have to publish it. You don't even have to send it to beta readers. That's not the important part. Starting something new is the key to growth and happiness. Keep writing. Take everything you've learned from this book into your next project, and your next. You'll be amazed at how much easier the next book is to write, and as your skillset levels up, the next one will be easier yet.

Let it Go?

I would never advise you to abandon a project halfway through a rough draft to start a new one. You'll learn more from finishing a draft than you will from quitting. Infinitely more. However, that being said, it's possible to finish a book, edit it to your satisfaction, incorporate beta feedback, edit again…and still have a novel that isn't ready for publication.

Some people call them drawer novels, or trunk novels, or novels under the bed. Every single professional novelist I've ever talked to or read interviews with has these beginning novels that are not published. I, personally, have three of them and I don't regret them one bit.

It's rare for an author's first novel to be published. Most authors publish their second or third. It's okay to learn. It's okay to practice. And it's far better to listen to your gut than to waste a year of your life querying and racking up a hundred rejections, or self-publish a novel that you *know* isn't ready yet. Such a book will only hurt your brand.

Listen to your gut. Truly listen. It's extremely hard to sort out ordinary fear of failure from deep-seated doubt that this project is any good, but it's okay to let early work go into your drawer. If any doubts linger in the back of your head, wait a bit, work on something else, and then see how you feel. Don't keep looping back, trying to make a book perfect. Work on your next project.

How Can You be Sure?

But let's say you're on the other end of that. Let's say you've revised the heck out of your book and you feel like it's ready to publish. In fact, you're almost certain. But how can you be sure? Like anything else in art, this is subjective, but I do have three suggestions and you're not going to like any of them.

First, can you sum up your novel in one sentence? Not a run-on sentence that's actually a paragraph. I mean, one sentence—around twenty words. Will that sentence intrigue someone enough to buy your book?

Second, if your book was published tomorrow, and it was at your local library and bookstore, do you know exactly which shelf it would be on? Are you sure? This means you know where your novel fits in the marketplace. Can you think of two or three comparable titles? I'm not talking about the bestsellers in your genre. Who are the midlist authors or capable indie authors whose books are similar to yours?

The third one is even more foolproof and you're going to hate it more. There is a switch that flips in a writer's brain when she's halfway through the *next* project that gives her perfect clarity about the last one. I can't explain it, but when you're halfway through book two, you will understand book one. When you're halfway through book three, you will suddenly "get" book two. It's mysterious, it's magical, but it's real.

What happens when that switch flips? Either

you realize your last book was fine, and that you nailed it, or you'll know exactly what went wrong with the previous book and you'll know exactly how to fix it.

I know you think I'm just making stuff up now, but I promise you this is real. So write to the best of your ability, revise as much as you can, and then start your next project. Continuing to move forward will pay off in multiple ways.

TEN

You Got This!

Reaching the end of the first draft is just the beginning for a writer. Revising your novel is a necessary and vital step. I hope this book has helped you look forward to revising your novel. You should enjoy this process. It's your golden opportunity to take that wonderful story you have in your mind and make it appear on the page exactly the way you intended.

It's true that revisions are hard and time consuming, but like all writing skills, revision gets easier the more you do it. With your first novel, you might find yourself doing several drafts, fixing one thing each time. With later novels, you'll need fewer drafts because with each pass, you're fixing multiple things at once.

And here's the best news of all. The more projects you finish, the less you'll need to revise. You'll start baking those "fixes" in right from the outset. That's the true beauty of revision. You'll learn so much from this process—tools you can take with you into your next project, and the next. And once those skills are in your writer's toolbox, they are yours for life.

One day, your novel will be accepted at a publishing house or you'll hire a freelance editor on your own before you indie publish. When that time comes, the editing process will be a breeze for you, because you've done most of the heavy lifting on your own.

The key is to work hard, trust your instincts, and keep your eyes on the prize—a finished book that you'll be proud of. A book that readers will love.

Acknowledgments

Special thanks to Bethany, Christine, Clif, and Michael for valuable advice.

A huge shout-out to the Ann Arbor District Library, and to my co-teachers Lara and Bethany. Special thanks to everyone who attended the Emerging Writers Workshop. I can't wait to see all your books on the shelves.

About the Author

Alex Kourvo loves books. She reads them, writes them, edits them, reviews them, and teaches other people how to write them.

Alex is an editor with over a decade of experience editing for small presses and private clients, and is the co-founder of the Emerging Writers Workshop at the Ann Arbor District Library, where she's been giving monthly writing classes since 2014. Alex's blog, Writing Slices, is exclusively dedicated to reviewing how-to books for writers. There are over 200 reviews on her site.

Alex lives in Michigan, in the perfect house on the perfect street in the perfect town. She loves key lime pie, puppies, sunbeams, and new books to read.

You can visit Alex on Twitter or Instagram, or find out more about her editing services at
    AlexKourvo.com

What's Next?

Ready to take your novel to the next level? Learn how to ramp up the stakes in your novel by reading:

No Hero Wants to Save the World: How to Raise the Stakes in Your Fiction

Every writer has been given the same advice countless times. In order to grip readers, you must raise the stakes. But what does that mean, and how do you go about doing that?

Story stakes come in three kinds: inner stakes, outer stakes, and personal stakes. The key to raising the stakes is first knowing the difference between the three kinds, and then knowing when to apply each one. And most important of all, knowing that heroes and heroines don't *want* the stakes raised. They are resisting danger at every turn, and unless there is something personal in the story pushing them to act, they will not cooperate with the excellent plot you've laid out for them.

No Hero Wants to Save the World is the guide you need to raise the stakes in a way that truly matters. You'll find what's most important to your characters, how to get them personally involved, and how to crank up the tension on every page. You'll discover the ideal time to reveal the true stakes of your story, and how to add in plot twists that work.

Alex Kourvo is an editor with more than a decade of experience helping writers. Under her guidance, beginners and award-winning authors have brought their careers to the next level. Now, she'll help you do the same. No matter the genre, this short manual gives you all the insight you'll need to write the novel that keeps readers turning the pages.

www.ingramcontent.com/pod-product-compliance
Lightning Source LLC
Chambersburg PA
CBHW051737290426
43673CB00101B/447/J